Praise the Lord, the God of Israel!
He has come to save his people.
Our God has given us a mighty Savior
from the family of David his servant.

(Luke 1:68–69)

The First Noel

Pauline
BOOKS & MEDIA

Library of Congress Cataloging-in-Publication Data

Roche, Maïte.
  [Plus belle histoire de Noël. English]
  The first Noel / Maïte Roche ; [translated by Marianne Lorraine Trouvé]. -- 1st North American ed.
      p. cm.
  ISBN 0-8198-2687-1
  1. Jesus Christ--Nativity--Juvenile literature. I. Title.
  BT315.3.R62713 2009
  232.92--dc22
                          2009011671

Scripture texts in this work are taken from *The Holy Bible: Contemporary English Version,* copyright © 1995, American Bible Society, 1865 Broadway, New York, NY 10023, and are used by permission.

Translated by Marianne Lorraine Trouvé, FSP

Originally published in French under the title *La plus belle histoire de Noël* by Groupe Fleurus, Paris, 2006

Copyright © Mame-Edifa, Paris, 2006

www.fleuruseditions.com

"P" and PAULINE are registered trademarks of the Daughters of St. Paul.

First North American edition, 2009

Published by Pauline Books & Media, 50 Saint Pauls Avenue, Boston, MA 02130-3491

Printed in Korea

www.pauline.org

Pauline Books & Media is the publishing house of the Daughters of St. Paul, an international congregation of women religious serving the Church with the communications media.

1 2 3 4 5 6 7 8 9   14 13 12 11 10 09

The First Noel

God sent the angel Gabriel
to announce wonderful news
to Mary,
a young woman in Nazareth.

Nazareth was the little village in Galilee
where Mary lived
with her family.
Mary loved God with all her heart,
and she waited trustingly
for the coming of the Savior
who would bring salvation
for all people.

Gabriel went to Mary's house
and said to her,
"Hail Mary, full of grace,
the Lord is with you.
God has chosen you among all women
to be the mother of Jesus, the Savior.
The Holy Spirit will come upon you."
Mary replied,
"I am the servant of the Lord."

Mary was engaged to marry Joseph,
who was a carpenter in the village.
One night, while he was sleeping,
the angel Gabriel appeared to him in a dream
and said,
"Joseph, Mary is going
to have a baby who is the Son of God.
You will give him the name 'Jesus,'
because he is the Savior."

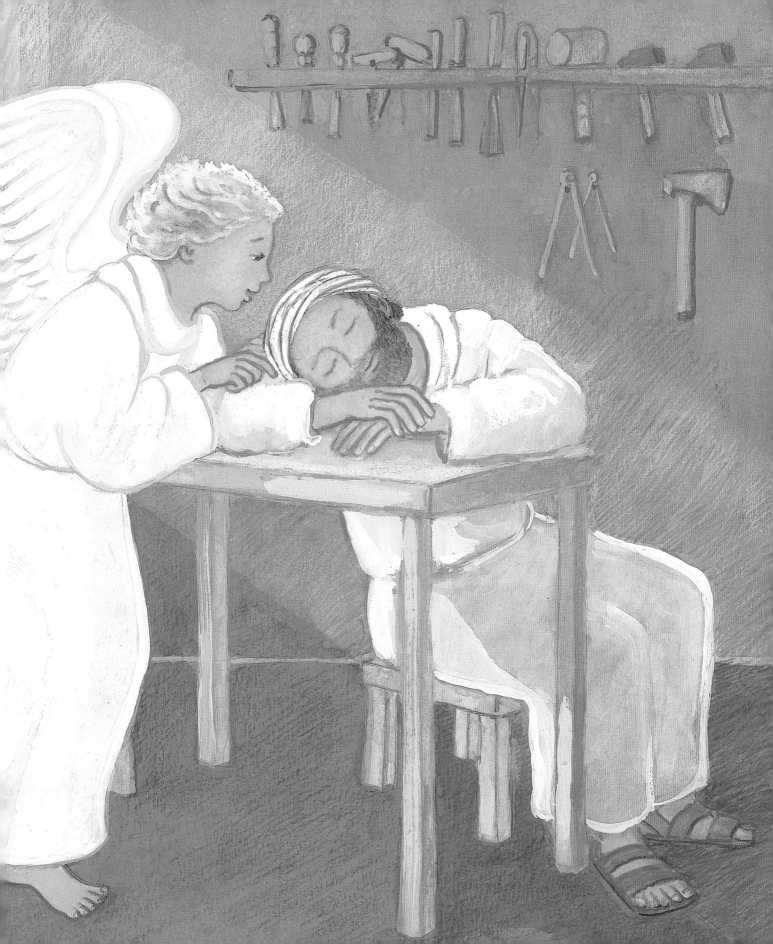

Joseph hurried to Mary's house.
He was very happy.
He now knew that God had chosen him
to love and protect Mary and Jesus.
How wonderful!

Mary and Joseph's wedding day arrived.
Their family and friends gathered together.

"Come sing and dance with us!"

The emperor Caesar Augustus had ordered
that everyone who lived in his empire must be counted.
Joseph and Mary had to travel to register
in Bethlehem, the town of Joseph's ancestors.
It was winter, and very cold.
A small donkey carried Mary.
Mary knew it was almost time for Jesus to be born.

When Joseph and Mary arrived in Bethlehem,
there was no room for them at the inn.
But someone showed them a cave
where there was a stable for animals.

In the middle of the night, Mary's Son was born.
Tenderly, she wrapped him to keep him warm.
Joseph said softly, "Jesus, you have nothing but a manger
for your cradle and a poor stable for your house,
but our hearts are filled with love for you,
the Son whom God has given us."

In the fields, some shepherds
were guarding their sheep. Suddenly a great light
began to shine, and they were frightened.
The angel of the Lord appeared to them
and said, "Do not be afraid!"

"I bring you news of great joy.
A Savior is born for you!
He is a little baby
whom you will find
in a manger in Bethlehem."

"Hurry! Go to see the little baby
who is born for you!"
The shepherds hurried to the manger.
In the sky, a multitude of angels sang with joy,
"Glory to God in the highest!
Peace to all people on earth!"
Heaven and earth were celebrating.
It was the first Noel!

The shepherds arrived in the stable and said,
"An angel told us that the Savior has been born here!"
"His name is Jesus," Joseph said.
Then the shepherds saw Jesus.
Peace and joy filled their hearts.

The shepherds left and sang praises to God.
"Rejoice! The Savior is born and we have seen him!"
Everyone who saw Jesus was filled with wonder.
Mary kept all these things in her heart.

In a faraway country in the East,
three wise men saw a brilliant new star.
"This is a sign that a great King has been born.
His light is bright! Let us go and adore him."

The wise men arrived at the palace of King Herod in Jerusalem.
Herod asked them, "Where is the newborn king?"
They answered, "He has been born in Bethlehem."

Herod was angry because he didn't want anyone else to be king. So he tricked the wise men into thinking that he wanted to worship Jesus, saying, "Go and find this king, then come back and tell me about him."

At Bethlehem, the wise men
were filled with joy.
They bowed down
to adore Jesus,
and they offered him precious gifts:
gold, myrrh,
and frankincense.

The angel of the Lord warned the wise men
not to go back to Herod's palace.
They went back home by another route.
Herod was very angry about Jesus,
and he ordered his soldiers,
"Go to Bethlehem
and look for all the babies
who might be Jesus."

During the night, the angel Gabriel
came to Joseph in a dream and said,
"Get up quickly and leave with Mary and Jesus.
King Herod wants to harm the baby."

Joseph led the small donkey
that carried Mary and Jesus.
Herod's soldiers
looked for Jesus during the night.
"Have faith; God is with us,"
Mary said. Jesus slept peacefully
in his mother's arms.

Joseph, Mary, and Jesus arrived in Egypt.
There, Herod could not harm them.
Mary and Joseph said,
"Blessed be the Lord
who has saved us!"

After some time, the angel Gabriel
appeared to Joseph and said,
"King Herod has died, and there is no more danger."
Joseph, Mary, and Jesus returned to Nazareth.
Their family and friends came to welcome them.
They were all so happy to be together again!

In Nazareth, Jesus grew up in his family.
The Holy Spirit was with them.
Mary said to him tenderly,
"Jesus, you have filled us with joy,
and you have shown us all
how much God loves us."

Pauline
BOOKS & MEDIA

The Daughters of St. Paul operate book and media centers at the following addresses. Visit, call or write the one nearest you today, or find us on the World Wide Web, www.pauline.org

CALIFORNIA
   3908 Sepulveda Blvd, Culver City, CA 90230   310-397-8676
   2640 Broadway Street, Redwood City, CA 94063   650-369-4230
   5945 Balboa Avenue, San Diego, CA 92111   858-565-9181

FLORIDA
   145 S.W. 107th Avenue, Miami, FL 33174   305-559-6715

HAWAII
   1143 Bishop Street, Honolulu, HI 96813   808-521-2731
   Neighbor Islands call: 866-521-2731

ILLINOIS
   172 North Michigan Avenue, Chicago, IL 60601   312-346-4228

LOUISIANA
   4403 Veterans Memorial Blvd, Metairie, LA 70006   504-887-7631

MASSACHUSETTS
   885 Providence Hwy, Dedham, MA 02026   781-326-5385

MISSOURI
   9804 Watson Road, St. Louis, MO 63126   314-965-3512

NEW JERSEY
   561 U.S. Route 1, Wick Plaza, Edison, NJ 08817   32-572-1200

NEW YORK
   150 East 52nd Street, New York, NY 10022   212-754-1110

PENNSYLVANIA
   9171-A Roosevelt Blvd, Philadelphia, PA 19114   215-676-9494

SOUTH CAROLINA
   243 King Street, Charleston, SC 29401   843-577-0175

VIRGINIA
   1025 King Street, Alexandria, VA 22314   703-549-3806

CANADA
   3022 Dufferin Street, Toronto, ON M6B 3T5   416-781-9131